Spirits Among Us

Jen Selinsky

Kindle Direct Publishing

ISBN 9798654103253

*Not every poem included in this book is dated in chronological order. This is not an oversight on my part. Rather, I have made changes and substitutions over the years.

-J.L.S.

I am enchanted by the trees

And how their leaves sway back and forth.

Nothing can take my eyes away from the sun

As it beats down pure golden rays of light.

Nature is so fascinating, but I can't admit

That I stay there too long.

My time is limited,

And my days are

Cut in half.

Who has the right to laugh at

What I have to say? *Touché!*

My arms are bound together,

But my legs are running free;

What has come over me?

Time hath its way

As it grabs hold

Of my soul.

God bless us, assigned as we are;

Someday, we'll go very far.

Long roads and smiling trees

Have all built a past on me.

Show me the direction in which to go

So that I may know how to live out

The rest of my life.

Govern me surely,

And please guide me

Through the strife.

2/12/00

I feel the same every time that you

Call my name.

Nothing changes, nothing's new;

Gotta hide all my feelings for you.

All the pain and all the sorrow

Will not be with me tomorrow;

Finding I can get away brightens up

My entire day.

The wheel still spins, and the cock still crows.

His face, with radiance, still glows.

The aftershine is upon us while

Borrowed favors just turn away;

Might we join in the fray?

I can clearly see that the storm's ignited

When all the clouds fall from the sky.

Oh me, oh my, my love has cost me my life!

So ends a year of turmoil,

And so begins another year of strife.

2/12/00

The Mad Man

The mad man claims he danced with me

At the last year's country fair.

I cannot see where he's coming from;

My opinion may not all be there.

He rolls his eyes and taps his heels

When he's had a little too much to drink.

I think I may be heading home now

To avoid the lunacy that awaits.

People sometimes wonder how much time

That I have left before I lose my insanity.

The mad man is going deaf.

2/12/00

Let me sing one more tune

Before the bar is closed for the night.

The only pain lies here in my heart,

My heart has secrets it can't tell.

Close the door and leave;

You're not here with me.

Please respect

My wish, (my wish)

And let me to myself.

Windows to the

World never let me see;

Curtains were always drawn.

What have you

Tried to hide, (to hide)

From my unsuspecting eyes?

Close the door and leave;

You're not here with me.

Please respect my wish, (my wish)

And let me to myself.

All odds bet against you

Now that I've told the world

Of your evil plan—

The plan to manipulate my mind.

Close the door and leave;

You're not here with me.

Please respect my wish, (my wish)

And let me to myself.

2/14/00

You know what I think of you,

That you have a place in my heart.

I have nothing else to say, and I shall

Continue with mine.

Before people start to suspect too much,

Let us go our separate ways.

We're through, and there's nothing

That you can do; just let me turn the page

To the next chapter.

I hope that something else is in store

For the poor, patient girl,

Who waits for her turn.

This world is overrun by people

Who are unfair to others.

I wish to depart the planet knowing

That I had at least one who seemed to care,

And He is up above, high in the hea'ns,

Is where the clouds of His Mind reside.

Maybe I'll be in one someday;

They put my face on a shining star.

3/3/00

I'm sorry to say that Ichabod has fallen

(For another girl, he's given her name).

Who's to be his Katrina now, some woman

Whom he hardly knows?)

He's cast me into the shadows, too far

From any light.

The headless horseman down the road,

Waiting to sever again.

And this time, I do not care,

And I hope that he shall win!

    Katrina is dead!

3/3/00

What ails me, my dear, is the fact

That you still don't care.

I was once presented to you,

So young and so fair.

Who's to say that I am wrong,

And what kinds of things did I not give?

I thought I gave my life to you,

And you sucked it in like a sieve!

Oh, believe me, I will move on,

But I do not know what to.

I have plans for myself that don't

Include the likes of you.

    Farewell…

3/3/00

All of God's Creatures

All of God's creatures, if meshed together,

Do not dare resemble the likes of you.

Their innocence is fragile, but none

Are quite as gentle and as true.

Your feats are captivating;

No description can match your eyes.

I can't believe that it took me

Twenty years to realize that God

Created a man especially for me.

I'll give you my heart, and whatever

Else you seem to need, as long as

Our love is guaranteed.

Oh, hold my hand, and I'll let you

Hold my heart.

Everything in my

Possession is also thine.

How would I continue on without

Your soul to keep?

You bring forth all the necessities

That this woman needs

In order to survive.

No longer do I have to strive just to

Keep our heads afloat;

I have you to present

With the utmost care.

3/4/00

You make me realize just how special

You are to me, and I don't know which

Words to use to express my gratitude.

May the Good Lord bless you

In many ways, and I hope that the feeling

Stays when others are in need of your help.

Please stay by me and

Let me take your hand,

Nothing can heal me now,

Except for your love.

My *imzadi is sent from above

I grow tired and can

Say no more words,

For my heart is

Pumping too much for me

To handle.

Poor, dependent me,

I've always been one

To indulge in self-pity,

Realizing that you are not

Always by my side.

But, nonetheless,

You have once taught me

How to love, a most valuable lesson

That one should live to learn.

I go now in peace, hoping that you haven't

Forgotten it all.

imzadi word taken from *Star Trek*, meaning true love

5/24/00

At last, I've returned from my most

Exhausting journey.

All the worst is over; most of all

My soul is free.

Just help me let the past be.

Miles and miles of the dusty road

All sprawl out in front of my face.

Oh, which direction should I choose,

And do they all go the same way?

I shan't walk any farther until

I'm guaranteed a place to stay.

My head throbs and aches;

Something tells me that this is not

Such a good idea.

My instincts brief me the same,

Only in less of a subtle manner.

What a pleasant grandeur,

I don't think I can make

It too much further,

For my head is throbbing

 And burning up inside.

So let me write out my

Last will and testament;

I know of some others who can

Benefit from my love.

I am fading fast and have no time

To finish what I need [to].

5/28/00

Art

Such soft blue eyes have set my

Heart a flame.

To get lost in them for hours,

To get a reflection back of myself—

I'd compare you to a painting,

But you have more dimension than that.

Fine words and sculpture could not

Even begin to immortalize you—

Not even close enough to do justice.

Oh, let me take you instead,

We can make note of our souls together,

For the splendid art of love cannot be

Conquered or destroyed.

5/30/00

Let me embrace you with my

Loving perspective.

I know all the secrets you

Try to keep, and I'm going

To conquer them—make you mine.

As the sun tries to control my moves,

Keep close, my fair friends.

Keep close, and let me know your

Final decisions.

  Only tomorrow can hold us

And include us in its path.

5/30/00

What just happened back there,

Could I possibly have lost my status?

Just a number of things could have

Gone wrong; I could have lost my

Mind for good.

So many emotions and thoughts

Make my mind just as numb as the others.

What has happened to my permanent

Control; I've gone thus far thru

My manipulation.

Everything is still a blur, can you find

A cure for what I'm feeling?

Confusion takes its course, and I feel

As if I got the short end of the stick.

Ho! What comes for me in the most

Haunting of hours?

Could it be the dour faces of those

Whom I despise?

Surely (I hope) not because I want to love

Those whom I fear.

6/2/00

I am fully grown,

But I am still immature at heart.

 How can I feel so alone, so scared;

Please explain what is going on!

 I don't want to live my life in constant fear,

And I want my mind to be void and clear

Of all the thoughts that would

Make me ill.

It seems the world has stood still,

Dead in the silence of man.

Do any of these people still care

To understand?

The laws are so simple, yet so far removed.

How was I supposed to know how soon

Things would fall apart, for this was

Someone else's work of art.

Let me claim back what is mine

So that I can go on knowing that things

Are just fine.

6/2/00

Epitaph for a Dead Sister

You're lost, little sister,

Hast thou gone out to peace?

[I've] mourned for you—

Nine long years—deceased.

How would life have been different?

How many less tears falling down

From our eyes?

Oh, so sweet—the young and innocent

Gone in a heartbeat.

 Thou precious life—

No more smiles exposing shiny,

White teeth.

Thou ebony hair reduced to ash,

And eyes of cinnamon brown-

Gone—no more souls to

Comfort and console.

No more flesh and blood, the

Warm feeling in my hand is GONE,

All cold.

Oh, how we three brothers shall

Miss you.

If time would have allowed,

You'd be thirteen years of age.

That number,

You'd be not in some cold grave—

Deteriorating away.

The memories are far too painful

Because I recall clearly that day.

The monsters were

High on the balconies,

Waiting for an easy kill.

They saw the innocent—

Determined to

Feast on some blood

And tears mixed.

The savage fiends fled as I fell

On my knees, and doves flew overhead.

My older eyes are now crying

And hoping you found your way upstairs.

God be with you and hold you in regard;

Here the earth still weeps for you,

And I pass by the stone which bears

Your name—the sweet smell of flowers

Fills the air, and I see you smile one more time.

6/5/00

Please let me know how to
Help you so that we may find the
Right way (and the truth).
I cannot give up
Such a destination;
Lord knows how much time we
Have left.
It could take days to find what we
Are looking for.
We'd strive and starve before the
Proper knowledge was obtained.
The days and journey add up
But, this time, it is all worth it.
I am going to gain the
Highest knowledge
To make myself
And the world proud.
Who's going to speak out loud?
Who's coming upstairs to make
The final bid?
We have to get our minds set
And go for our

Learning while the

Information's still hot, for this

Is the last chance

For the truest education

That we've ever got.

6/23/00

Does the beating of the heart

Cause one to make rash decisions?

I can know no other explanation

For what I feel inside.

Such a harsh price to pay—

To make so many others suffer

Is a sin.

Where should I begin?

There was the time that I was given

The dice, and my hand came up

Not exactly as I planned.

I panicked at the wrong time;

I should have given a better explanation

As to why I had to leave—

Only something that a fool could achieve.

I hang my head in sorrow and pray

For no more evil to come.

   Could it be too late?

I'm afraid nothing could tell just yet.

6/24/00

Could you be the one I'm looking for?

I've searched the night time through

And spun my heart around.

The piercing arrow of Eros

Has finally penetrated my soul?

I'm not absolutely sure this time,

But things may have taken a turn.

Suspicion of my feelings has

Temporarily led me astray.

6/24/00

Three Destinations

The straight path divides into three

Different directions; which one

Should I follow?

The one who has raised me

Is so loving and so kind,

But it seems as if

My feet cannot

Leave the ground.

Hence, bring the other two in

So that more fighting can begin.

Selfish needs or selfish love?

I can run swiftly into the woods,

Never to be seen again.

Oh, stop this

Senseless fighting!

I should be the

One to have any say.

My life shouldn't

Have to revolve

Around these three,

For my happiness

Keeps me in the game.

And, if any of them cannot

Be satisfied, then walk right off!

I can surely find another way around.

6/26/00

I remember the day just like it was

Yesterday; thy beautiful fate

Concealed—so young!

But immortality, is it such a price

To pay when the beauty of your youth

Still lives on?

Some think you brilliant, and others

Think you mad.

Only choose the few which matter to you;

Your mind alone can determine the past.

Golden hair, eyes full of promise,

And ears full of delight.

The muses count your very last words

And release them into the air.

Must I stare into your grave and pretend

That you are me?

We should not try to trade places

So that everything can, [be] let be.

*in memory of James Douglas Morrison

7/3/00

My way of life could get ugly

When the smile is stripped right off my face.

Given the place and time of my valentine;

The chapter has turned back a page,

And I sit and wonder when it will

Be my destiny to fulfill the needs

Of those who are trying to achieve

A sound goal.

The smoldering furnace allows us

Hardly any air to breathe.

My speech is growing shorter, and my

Once-keen eyes have nothing good

At all to perceive.

Yes, all it takes is the disappearance

Of one smile, to set my mind on rage—

The insatiable thirst of a sage.

7/20/00

Old Age

Objects and products can outlast us
In all our lives; just think of the things
A person uses in a day.
Some antiques have been around for
Several hundreds of years, and here
Our bodies lie as corpses—already
Reduced to dust and returned to
The earth.
But the grandfather clock still stands
In our living room, with new dust
To settle on it and more flesh
And blood to consume.
Why can't humans
Be just as valuable
As the old coins that sit on the tray?
I'm going to get old someday,
And I'll be stuck
In a pen with many
Others my age.
Left to rot and degrade, no one will

Be near to complain

We're not as valuable as

We'd like to claim,

Even though we've

All had a chance to live.

7/20/00

All teary-eyed, looking defeated,

The poor soldier strives to get home.

But no family is waiting, not much

Anticipating, not even a girl

To call his own.

You can see that this man needs a place

To rest his weary head.

Perhaps all the horror is only a dream,

And all those he cares for

Are surely not dead.

But, to his dismay, he wakes from sleep

A day later, and nothing has changed.

To appease the great hater,

Driven by madness and grief,

The hero strikes a match to

Burn his house down,

And all the great memories are ablaze

Before his eyes.

A loss and tragedy;

No one should have

To suffer, yet he is

No one now and unsafe

From the consuming flames.

Oh, the sad games

That war can play (with us)

When we have our backs turned,

Away from the light.

7/20/00

Good fellows, will you not show us the way

Out through the forest and into the light of day?

For, you see, we're quite tired from the fray.

Splendid feasts are awaiting us as ordered

By the king 'cause we slew the beast

That brought us here when the tide ebbed

Close to heart.

The sailors fell apart, and we picked up

From where they left off.

So you see, good fellows, we withstood

The test of time.

You can lend us your ears in accordance

To the rhyme.

Oh, hear our song and give us some place

To rest so that we can carry on and do everything

That we said.

7/22/00

How can I listen to you

When I can't even listen to myself?

All the words try to assuage me,

But they just fly out of my head.

Am I dead to the world and all

That's surrounding?

My senses have me trembling in fear

Because I can no longer hear the

Simple reason of sanity.

Instead of soft words, it's more like

Thunder, striking horror into the hearts

Of those who are tame.

[I can take] no more of this irrational pain;

Let me out just a few blocks underneath

The door before my very head caves in

With the feeling of doubt.

I feel like crying out to anyone, or anything,

Who has the heart to hear my once-

Imaginary plea.

7/22/00

My love is destined to be my petty hate;

Something's wrong with this fate.

The narrow halls of this depression

Are helping me to keep the books.

And, irrelevant as it may sound, I see

The attention is kept by looks.

Anything to despair is nothing, until it's done.

I hope the evil army's had its fun because

We shall depart from the building and

Into the sky.

Oh me, oh my, the clever stand

Has left his suit.

Shall I return it to him, even though

The point is moot?

Yes, my love has turned into an enemy,

And my hate has become an ally.

See why I cry now.

7/22/00

I met you in some kind of dream,

I don't know how long ago—

Intriguing words and faded memories.

Light shone on your face, and it didn't

Look quite the same.

How horrifying! Your form has

Changed completely.

Monstrous holes cover the cheeks

That reside on your once beautiful face.

Jagged teeth and sunken eyes, oh,

How your appearance frightens me!

But your words are so intriguing.

Erotic laughter and new tracks to

Fill my mind.

I finally found the time to drive myself

Madly in love.

And just to make sure things stay

The same, I'll be keeping track of my name

Because everything is still new to me;

It's all meant to be.

7/24/00

The days have all passed and

Yielded to the moon.

[The] initiation of the tribes

Is going to start soon.

Anticipation glowing, faces burn

Into the night.

Please speak to me, dear friend;

I will try my best to put an end

To whatever is ailing you.

'Tis the night that wants me to

Come closer and grab you by the soul.

These words are about to devour me whole.

Consuming minds wander the hallway

And look for innocent victims on

Which to prey.

9/2/00

Crashing thru the wilderness,

Blue eyes are shining bright.

I desire to put you inside my soul;

The darkness overwhelms me

As I try to come closer to my goal.

Where are you?

Oh, I'm floating in the unconscious,

Where no one dares to be awake.

Follow the snake that slithers

Down the undulating path.

9/2/00

Is her pale white skin so tantalizing

That it gives you wanton dreams?

I don't know quite what you

See in her, or is the truth still so

Hidden from your eyes?

I'm just here to try to save you,

No matter what your senses

Might say.

She may aim to lead you down

The wrong path.

And, no guiding light can save you,

Unless you can find some kind

Of blessing—an angel to see you

Through the darkness.

And I could be your salvation

To kiss your eyes and let the

Light shine through your soul.

She can only corrupt it

With her devil's kiss

And black poison

From the mouth

Which she speaks lies.

Please let me be the one!

9/2/00

Oh, you'd better hurry up, darling,

Before all the wedding bells stop ringing.

Do you really think that this idea

Of yours is good for me, or do you

Only want to wallow in your

Contentment to be?

For I have plans of my own,

My dear, and a

Marriage [our marriage]

Is nothing I care to celebrate.

But, give me your

Thoughts, and fill my head

With ideas so that I know.

I can avoid them

With a glare—the silver stare.

The chapel is waiting, but I know not

Who's inside.

Your ring thinks to

Capture me in a dress

You find so pure.

Am I running through the corridor?

Aha! You didn't make it, and my dress

Fades back to manila.

The bells stop ringing and, this time,

It's forever.

But your state of mind's improved,

As you finally let me go.

9/2/00

Am I the woman you so secretly desire,

And are you the man who has set my

World on fire?

A sudden interest has captured me,

And it's not going to let me go

Anytime soon.

I said I loved you, but it's only fascination,

Like the way you put your lips to my hand.

You're a contribution to my lifetime of friends;

But, be cautioned, I may just try to take you away

To a place of which I call paradise.

But don't mind the others who are here

For my pleasure, too.

I'd have half a mind to remove them

If they were to create such a wild stir.

In my idealized land of hedonism,

Such utter nonsense shall never occur!

9/6/00

[My dream's] to have every man

Fawn over me.

A sex-type goddess, just appropriate

For the age.

Famous courtesan—the one and only

To make them all melt is my game.

It may sound pompous, and it may

Sound crass, but my desire is

Much too strong to throw away.

I can't give up the impossible dream;

My head needs something to occupy

The time in fantasy.

Do my thoughts appeal to you,

Or am I just making up some to

Fill my hopeless mind?

But let me live my lascivious lifestyle;

Only in true happiness will I find [myself]

To be in a proper state of mind.

So no one can disturb me in my bliss;

Does it really have to amount to all of this?

9/6/00

Am I just some kind of toy,

An emotionless thing with which to play?

All your glass is broken, and your

Wood is rotting away.

[You've] no time for metal; rust has

Done its job today.

Just give you flesh and blood

With human breasts and eyes.

When will the time come for you

To realize that I have a right to think

And act for myself?

 The flesh and blood have started

A rebellion.

 No longer a second-class citizen

Do I have to be.

The time has come for me to rise

And put an end to the sin that I have received

 With nothing else conceived.

9/6/00

Why should I put all my trust

In something that I hate?

My life is here, in shambles, all because

Of a permanent glitch, and all I want

To do is curse and swear.

Oh, damn the complications and all

My frustrations!

This time, I let go

And spit in your face;

Right in the eyes lies

The hatred of my past—

Melancholy because

My throbbing heart

Won't stop.

Alas! Time's running out, and so is

My patience with the machine.

How wretched and feeble-minded

Such evil creatures can be—

Consuming our money and stabbing us

In the backs of the land of the free

And the home of the brave.

 Do I venture too far in my guess,

Or do I have, or are we all just

A corporate slave?

9/6/00

Mental Issues

Some people may think that I have issues
And that I live in a sick and perverted world.
But, who really knows, they may actually
Be right.
  Just because I am not the same,
The world still calls out to me
A recluse—high in my haven,
And faraway from those who oppose me.
Can I really be so depressed that I
Juggle my fate in the hands of deception?
 Perception is as perception can receive.
Mine is so mind-boggling distorted.
That I think a smile is closer to a frown,
And the laughter in my head will
Proclaim me as [being] dead, unless I can
Find something to throw away my shame
The mental issues may never go away.

9/6/00

Please let me sende my love;

Fore you, it does not ende.

'Tis why I push this pen

In hopes you will remember mee.

At first glance, you captured my soul

And plaid the strings of my hearte

But doth no music and arte.

Compare with whate you have

Given to mee.

Though it seems years since

Laste I saw you, my love shall

Remain just the same.

In time wille reclaime

What we have seene before.

'Ere comes the dawn, but no magic's

Without you.

The sunne's rayes no longer

Interest me, nor do skyes

Of splendid hue.

So have a byrd fly hither, anon.

Oh lette it be a dove so I canne

Heare its sweet songe.

Just from thy lips, such tender

Words do flow.

They ne'er let me goe to bee

Alle on my owne.

My hearte is al'ays with thee,

Ee'n though I must sing alone.

9/7/00

Lette not thy strife interfear

With our love—e'en the darkest

Temptation canne spoil what our

God haveth for us.

Cain hath mark'd upon his body

The punishment which he

Canne not escape.

Jelesy and murdur hath done

A terrible cryme—but love canne

Prevente it from happening in thy place

And in our time.

9/7/00

Your splendour hath given me

The truth beyond the past,

So, now, all can see what lies ahead.

No pathes unbroken, and no days

Ending in fury.

I'll only be so peaceful as too

Lende you my hearte this once,

But my undying promise shall

Staye with me for all eternitee.

In written agreement do I have

Your solemn word?

You must give whole-heartedly,

No contract may you breake,

For I shall have to chase you outside.

My realm and cause you hallucinations

Of your greatest mistake.

10/16/00

Our immortal souls can lift us above

All our physical boundaries

And alleviate the tearing of the flesh.

No special wounds can conceal us now;

Our spirits are bound toward heaven.

And unkind words let no shedding of blood,

For they do not have the power to open up

Any wound to let blood flow from the veins.

Only our God can protect us from the

Harsh realities found within…

10/19/00

To a Girl Who I Once Knew

Though it's been years since I've seen

Or heard from you, I have not forgotten

That you're still around.

No words have been exchanged,

And no thoughts are much in common.

You're probably all successful

In the starting of your new life.

But I think of it as

Only being yesterday,

As we used to play

Out in our backyards.

So many times, you tried to get me

In trouble, and so many times I cried

Because it wasn't fair!

I looked up to you and thought your word

Was as good as gold.

No one could have made you seem bad,

No one could have taken you away.

Now, we live such separate lives,

And I wonder what you're doing right now.

[You're] probably married with a

Small child or two,

A dog or a cat, depending on your taste.

But, I shall not forget you, though long ago

It was…

*dedicated to Jenelle Trapold

10/24/00

Twenty-Seven

8/27/04

Funny I should look opposite

And see you.

You, who have been in my thoughts

Occasionally in the last four years.

If you did not have those things

Back then, then I suppose you

Have come close to achieving—

Obtaining them right now.

In my wildest dreams, I should like

To think that you would still talk to me,

If ever we cross paths again.

You have grown up so normal,

Whereas eccentricity is my middle name.

I suppose that this is all fine since we

Have yet to actually coincide.

In all things meant to be, we shall certainly see…

*dedicated to Jenelle Trapold

8/27/04

For whom should I weep

And wet my pillow with tears?

Should it be my mother,

Who tries to have her way;

My beloved, or my confidant,

Against each other and doubling me

In pain?

Endless nights, I wonder what

Has gotten into me.

My eyes are shut, and blood spurts out

Because my poor heart aches—

Deciding who I choose

To "be my best"

Is a painful task indeed!

Or, should it be my sister or father,

Who think they both

Have the best in mind;

They silence the tongue of the official

But speak of the other two cast in flames.

And my darling girl cannot hear me,

Nor does she have anything to say.

Oh, make me independent

Of any and all

The underlings, for my

Tears shall dry only

Under a certain kind

Of command.

10/24/00

God's Word has its way of delivering

The best of things.

Bitterness is put aside

Because all the mortals don't matter,

For He loves us all, each and every one,

Though hurt and pain are abundant in our veins.

Whatever suffering we encounter during this life,

We are sure to make up for in heaven.

I know my faith is not the best that it could be,

But I give my heart in all that I do.

Each day I learn to love so much better,

For that is the reward which God has given me!

10/24/00

Hello, my dear, you cannot

Resist me.

Powerless the struggle and wasteful

The time, I'll be in your mind,

And there's nothing you can do;

I've got a hold on you.

You cannot escape the ropes which

Bind you; everything should be

Perfectly clear.

Can you not hear the realization

That's eating away at your brain?

All your senses are numbed,

But time's called back no fury.

I have this much to say when you're

Squirming in my arms; I kind of

Like the feeling.

You undulating and trying to be free,

It makes me feel all the more powerful,

But I will not let you be!

10/24/00

" 'Tis you who are intelligent,

And not I," stated the queen,

But little did she realize what

That phrase would come to mean.

Through many

Kingdoms I've searched

And never found the key.

Those times are lost in the frozen tundra;

We'll just have to let things be.

O', let me cry for the bleeding martyrs,

Who gave their life for me.

I would have done

The same thing, too,

Except I'd never be free.

Tons of bricks have fallen onto the

Second story floor.

I lift my weary head to

See who's at the door.

Chimes on clocks do ring—

Solo mia in the spring.

Death in wonder you bring,

Hosiery to thighs doth cling.

No more time is left for me to explain;

I must start the race all over again.

Until we meet some other time,

I say, our eager hearts can never join in

The fray.

10/24/00

I know with what I am to

Concern myself, and the afterlife

Is not looking forward to me.

I want to be humble, here on earth

(I am) at peace with nature only to find

The innocent land.

Which is why I live in the country;

The city is far too

Corrupt for my being.

Oh, let me celebrate

Life and friendship

With the very wine I put to my lips!

Make me not go out into the fields

Of work today.

Time is far too precious to waste,

Toiling over such laborious tasks.

While trying to sew the land,

Fussing and cursing is not the ideal.

It would spoil my temperament

Far too much.

My disposition ruined

By such nonsense!

Instead, I meditate through the mind,

The peace I strive to achieve.

Out in the garden, my pretty tiger-

Lilies bloom, and I think to myself

How lucky a man am I!

10/23/00

Open areas reveal ghastly faces,

And I hide myself from the haunting images,

Which flicker across the wall.

That is all I have to fear, but everything's

So constant and far too clear to see.

It might as well be me who gets cast

Into the pit of despair, for all my life

I have sinned.

What can I do to mend my awful ways?

I've given my life to the most important factor.

I pray every night for salvation, but how

Am I to know just what I'll receive?

Many people can breathe, knowing how well

They are about to do.

I know I'd be lost without you.

12/1/00

I realize sleep is coming over my eyes,

But I know I can do nothing from

The place in which I lie.

I'm trapped

With a bunch of people I'm supposed

To call my friends.

This torment never ends; it just

Keeps on gnawing at my gut.

Like a poor, starving creature,

I'm doomed to wander the ruins alone.

Civilization has lost a hold of me, as

An acorn has fallen from a tree.

Meet the eyes of curiosity as they

Are able to shut—with no resistance at all.

I call and call for the cure as my

Heartstrings race and race for the door.

Long fingers searching for the handle,

As they run themselves over the rusty lock

Alas! I cannot fall asleep right now

Because of the horrors that consume my mind.

12/1/00

How could you admire some people—

So vile with their interests and

So crude in their ways?

The land is shaved for any of those opposing,

Could I be a part of that group?

Shhh… No more questions, it's time

To close those pretty eyes.

Waiting for the temporary paradise

(To escape the endless amount of pain).

All of this is driving me insane!

Was I forced into something that

I cannot escape?

This place makes my stomach turn,

But my mind has time to wander free.

Oh, bring me back to the good old days,

When I was young and fancy-free.

How my mind dwelled on such simple thoughts;

Most every word was filled with glee.

12/4/00

I reach my hand out to you,

In hopes that you may need it someday.

Oh, give the fresh wounds a little

Time to heal, and watch me patiently

With those anticipating eyes.

Your new fascination lies in my direction;

I am trained to take you in.

Long-awaiting, the arrival of the

Golden wrath.

Shower of a god, and the sun shines

Down in my face.

Rain is far from reaching my boundaries

That day will come, that day will soon

Reach my senses.

Numbing my skin from the harmful elements,

I grow wings from my shoulders and fly

Far away…

12/4/00

Reassure yourself that you are not a man.

It was just another loss—"drunken"

Response of a hedonistic pleasure,

Thus the trembling's not over; my lips

Have parted with fear.

Oh, but the flesh looked so good,

And I wanted to take a dive,

But all I was doing was wading.

So sweet and new to my eyes,

Hands go out of control when curious.

But, was I that mean to you?

I can understand why you're so harsh;

A woman's heart is much less willing

To forgive because a man's is so absent—

It is much less easy to offend.

Except there are a certain few…

And, now, I must find

Peace with myself

Silence the lust that went

Through my fingers

And put my conscious mind to sleep.

I need to recharge my brain with happiness

Before I so long suffer to

Battle with the disease.

12/4/00

I need to get away; all room here

Is too close for comfort.

Too close! I need to have space to breathe.

Concealing my thoughts, how unhealthy

A way to live.

Let me get my words out, and fly

Them through the air.

Diseased and riddled, my hands are

Not the same.

What has become of them; are they

Corrupt from the fall?

I did not know that my mind could

Be the same—plagued with such confusion.

Have I done my penance yet?

The baggage, it's too heavy to carry

Any farther.

My days are numbered along with the

Pages on which I write.

I'd hate for it to be too late to make amends;

My poor little heart has had all that it can take.

12/5/00

There's no need to acknowledge my existence—

The world would be so much better.

This rogue needs to be silenced.

No further interruptions; let the ceremony proceed

A joyful day for all.

All of those who do not kiss the grave—

The cold and chiseled stone.

The skies hardly light with the morning sun;

Let me retreat to my sanctuary.

Worldly possessions all left behind

Could it only be you—the one who wants

To join me?

Hands are clammy, and your skin turns to flakes.

Close to being silenced, I let loose

From your grasp.

No need for two people falling

The final hour nears without much

Time left over.

Farewell, until we meet again,

In the unseen…

12/5/00

We're the ones who are standing

In their way (the most talked about of them all).

A goddess close to the sun—

A god who's farther behind, reaching out.

Sometimes, we can see them in backyards

With our families.

How beautiful their bodies, dominant

With colossal size.

But their faces are frowning, so many

Light years apart.

With our parties and gatherings,

We are smiling from the amount of

Our success,

While two lonely beings

Seek to find each other

And make something beautiful

Confusion.

That's what we give

Them so they can further

Put off meeting.

Maybe we should

Be demolished, or put

On the outer regions.

How would we enjoy

Our parties out there?

Their glows may become

Brighter with their smiles.

12/5/00

So many changes have occurred in the

Past few days.

Who would have thought that my life

Could be so interesting?

No longer a fresh and clean maiden;

No, I haven't been that way for years,

Swallowed in my own blood and guilt.

I'm about to be drowned and choked

As I go on further down.

Now, it's boiling mad.

Nothing is good right now, and I don't

Know if it ever will be… again.

12/5/00

Are you glad to have spat in my face

And kicked me down the stairs?

Now I feel terrible, but I suppose that

(That) was the point.

We shouldn't fight over a mishap

Or a man, friends should be

Much stronger

Than that.

However, I let you know that I suffer

These repercussions

So that you may

Be content and feel right.

A stronger mind should

Come from this all,

But my body is progressively

Becoming weaker—

Consuming itself in its fury.

I need to get out and release

My pent-up emotions.

Although the snow will not mix

Well with my blood, the hounds

Will still come for the smell.

Red on top of white and melting

Through to the crust of the earth.

Perhaps it will sink in even farther

Down to the mantle, and the core

Will consume it with greedy hunger.

12/5/00

Pleased to see you outside

And still alive,

Amidst the rain, and amidst

The harsh weather.

I found that I should not do

So well under these conditions,

But you are a different kind of animal.

Something, I don't know what—

So majestic when you transport

Yourself from point A to point B.

It only adds to the mystery that

Encapsulates the things that

I want to know.

I am not alone; there are others

Who inquire as well.

8/27/04

I must get out of this dreadful place,

It reminds me all too much of hate

The pent-up hostility—no window

To the outside world.

History cannot allow me to repeat it;

God knows that I can't and will not

Do as it's told.

Now that I am starting to remember,

There's so much more that I want to forget.

Leave it behind in the harsh winter winds;

Blow it away.

Waiting for the spring and all the

Plants to germinate—recreate.

Long-forgotten will everything be,

Just like the time that burns right

Through the pages,

Gone.

12/5/00

I take the cyanide, mixed with the

Undetected beverage.

I stopped pretending just a day ago.

No use in playing these games;

No use in pretending you care.

I know the truth,

And I feel the despair.

So, good night, my darlings;

I hush myself with the cruel wind

Howling at my back.

No more sound from my mouth,

But my body still remains.

You can clean

Up the mess later,

Unless the wolves

Decide to have

An early feast.

A Merry Christmas, indeed!

Bellies are full, content with

Meat and wine.

Yawn and stretch and lay down

For a quick nap.

And then you're off for the

Next delicate morsel—merely leftovers

From the harvest.

But beware of the traps ahead—

The fine pilgrims with their gear.

12/5/00

We have just enough food to

Spread itself around.

Side dishes, complete with anger,

Hurt, innocence, and grief.

But the main entrée is guilt,

With which I continuously

Fill my plate.

You'll have nothing of the sort,

The two of you

Looking so sweet.

How could I prepare such a feast

(With) the main

Dish touched only

By myself?

Congeniality and side dishes are

Complimenting each other—

No amnesia to spread itself around

With the wine glasses all empty.

The bottles have been recycled,

And the labels were

Thrown in the trash.

Guilt fills up my belly.

Now all I want to do is sleep,

Sleep, sleep, sleep.

Yes, let's all take a nap in hopes

That the new year will come

And wipe the slate clean…

12/5/00

The engine hums and purrs

With such precision.

Shall we go for a ride,

It's a horrid day for walking.

Take me places that I've

Never been before,

And I'll look out the window

To see where we are and

Where we've been.

Your company gives me

Great pleasure;

The trip's so

Much more

Exciting with you.

Let's take the whole day to

Put our troubles behind us.

Let's take a long car drive,

Three or four hours of time.

People may worry

(About us)

When we are gone,

But that's OK,

As long as we know

We're all right.

We can throw away the rest of the

Night together—

Just you, I, and Ol' Smoky.

12/5/00

Aha!

This is it;

This marks the end

Of an era.

Something that I wanted,

Yet not the relief.

Once I am finished,

I wonder what kinds

Of things will happen

To make my mind think

About these days.

And what I am to achieve—

Nervousness and great

Anticipation all rolled up

Into one.

I'm sure that others

Would feel the same.

If it were they who

Had all this coming

Up for them.

8/27/04

I know how you feel;

I've been down the

Same road before,

Alcohol and drugs.

Do you want to walk

Through walls?

Let me into your mind;

There is no secret that you

Can hide from me.

C'mon, I know that you

Have some serious issues.

I've been to the same

Valley before.

I know how you act

And think.

Take some advice from

The expert.

C'mon, c'mon, I know

How you FEEL!

12/15/00

The great resurrection

Of an old fad, which has

Yet to reach those who

Have no clue of its existence.

Someone must know what

I am thinking, otherwise,

I am wasting all this

Precious time, which could

Be spent delivering something

To the other unsuspecting souls,

Who have no clue to stay behind

And watch what unfolds.

They all want to witness,

As the fanatics say, "phenomenon."

Along with I, who will be

Standing in the foreground

While directing the entire process.

8/27/04

You have no choice in the matter;
You're coming with me to make
Our lives complete.
 Just try to protest and say you know
What's the best for you.
 Your arguments will do you no good;
I can be just as mean and forceful
When convinced to go in the other
Direction—trust me when I say that
It's better to keep your mouth shut
And go along with my plan.
I'll hold your hand and guide you
Through all the gory details.
Your naive eyes should be spared
Of such harsh reality.
Such delicate brains—evil is intent to
Feast upon them.
Do not hesitate to make me
Your leader, and we'll travel to a land
Across the sunken sand.

12/8/00

Now that I've torn my way through

The pages and seen what they had to offer,

I can clearly say I'm satisfied

With the content found within.

Such a fine thing rarely exists—

To look for the finest can only cause

You to strain, unless you know how to

Seek it.

Prepare to become immersed in such culture

Where the everyday is not so mundane.

The literature, people would give

Anything for these talents.

They'd look up to you and smile

With such a graceful air, begging to take requests.

Wanting to hear the ground opening,

I blink my eyes and wonder where

Everything went.

Time grows shorter and shorter, but not enough

To fulfill my needs.

12/8/00

How bothersome the situation,

Such the inconvenience sucks me in

Why must I be put under these

Circumstances?

Give me some choice in the matter.

Only to have been on this planet

For twenty-two years

  Feels like an eternity,

So let me live the last few moments

Of my youth in peace.

Before I run out of ripe ink,

We must write the scroll of declaration—

Claiming such innocence to the

Constituents of the past.

Falling asleep in the prison cell,

My past makes sure that I will

Be all right.

Suddenly! An alarm goes off.

I realize where I am, and my

Solemn dream is over.

12/8/00

57

Did you think that I would forget

All about you when it's your day

To celebrate? 57!

 Such a beautiful man—left behind

A beautiful corpse.

Sleeping through the ages—unharmed by

The decaying life.

We still love you here—

Doing things in your remembrance

And letting the legend live on.

A brilliant figure to celebrate

Such sex appeal and posterity.

Today, you would have been 57,

Would your fame

Be affected by all this?

Maybe it's better

That you lie asleep

And uncorrupted, where everyone

Strives to be like you.

The pressure of the

World off your back.

Rest, dear child, rest up.

Hush now, and don't worry

About the fact that you would

Have grown older—such a shame.

*dedicated to Jim Morrison

12/8/00

Philosophy for Blake

This is the man, who lived

To start something extraordinaire.

My, such bravery it took to defy

The everyday convention and deliver

Matters from his own mind—his own hands.

He was visited by an angel, who held

Direct orders from God not to defy

These certain things, only he should

Express them through written word.

Some people just were not ready

For his open-mindedness, which set

The world on fire!

*dedicated to William Blake

8/28/04

You say you don't want to

Fall in love, how awful

Could it be?

Answering the questions

Which I have pondered

So many times before

Can only mean one thing—

The answers are not of

The highest quality.

You claimed to have had some

Bad experience, but this only

Leads me to believe that you've

Had none at all—that only

Fear of heartache holds you back,

But I can relate; yes, I can relate.

8/27/04

Unsettled—

Are the contents of my stomach,

Even though I have not

Eaten a thing for hours.

What has made this

Come on all of a sudden?

I thought that I have been

Very careful in controlling

My anxiety and the kinds

Of foods that I ingest.

I have to keep myself in shape

In order to escape the pressure;

I have to keep in shape so that

I can eliminate the pain,

Before it comes to manipulate me

In its cruelty.

I must get rid of all this!

8/27/04

Take me out of here

So that everything

Else can change.

 I don't want it to be the same.

The last few years have been lost—

All in one shallow plea.

But, I've learned my lesson and

Cracked my head hard on the

Bottom concrete floor.

Blood spurts out of my brain.

Yes, I've learned my lesson

I don't want to go back there.

No, at least give me some more

Time to myself.

Could this all be some kind of

Hallucination—

Only the good kind that I never

Want to go away.

A name…

But it's still not far enough back

I need to go further!

Ten more days without that name

And any others to

Which it's connected.

Bye-Bye, oh, fair, old world.

 Don't wait up for me, because the light

Will always be on…

12/20/00

Lock me up and throw away the key;

This rush of hedonism has clot my brain.

A brilliant man and a lost little girl—

Two souls who know nothing better to do.

Because I'm starting to forget almost

Everything that falls after the year 1995,

Forget the unforgiven.

The gap has closed the window to my memory;

What kinds of things would I have to

Sacrifice to travel back in time

To my dear old friend, who has always

Been there for me?

But my new friend still grows much stronger.

Relax and let me pick up from where I left off

Because the two of you combined are just like

Oil and water.

No desire to mesh, uncomplimenting

Toward each other.

You both have your counterparts galore.

12/20/00

Back on Track

Heading out
On the final part
Of my adventure.
So unorganized,
I feel I must put
These things back
In place so that
I can
Make a good
Impression—
Do what
I need to.
People are
Depending
On me to have
Thought out some
Kind of plan so
That I will not
Be destitute once
I am through

With this massive

Epic.

8/28/04

Shh… don't talk to me right now

Because I don't want to ruin

The moment.

 Such fine intimacy—

We'll go about our

Business tomorrow

And talk of serious things.

But, right now, let us just hold

Each other and stare at the blue

In the sky.

We have a long day ahead of us;

Relax and relish the moment.

Sooner or later,

We'll wish that we

Had taken advantage of our silence.

Laborious tasks will burden us;

Other people are

Going to make us

Do things according to their way,

But let us not think of

Such unpleasantries

Right now.

Even as the sky turns to reveal a

Lighter hue, we'll ignore the fact

That time is slipping away.

No one can disturb us in our

Safe haven before the full light of day.

12/30/00

I can no longer do this

Kind of business

Because inspiration has left me

Without a hint of a clue.

This state disgusts me,

And it will

Continue to do so even more.

I cannot stand the frustration—

So much anger built up inside

But too little energy

To do anything

About it.

Oh, damn this world of aggravation!

And in it, I can find no garden.

The fruit cannot

Grow off dead trees.

No production or harvest has seen

Its way to my door, so I set out

To find something

Worth seeing.

Such terrible knowledge found me

Nothing I could use.

Alas! My works may now be

Revered as hideous.

Like the carnival creature, who rears

Forward its shameless head.

This part is something that I dread…

12/31/00

Have you ever smelled human flesh

On fire?

(It has) the same morbid odor of a

Flaming bag of roasted peanuts.

Too nasty for any beast to endure,

It would be best advised to say far away,

Away from the flames roasting your minds.

What great fuel all of you can provide;

The fire loves to feast on human anxiety.

Any bad emotion just adds to the pile—

Reduced to ashes to clean out the dust.

Remember the burning flesh and how

Many people have had their bodies sacrificed.

The smell too awful for anyone to bear.

You cannot tell another living soul,

For some things have to be experienced

First-hand.

1/1/01

Sleep

I'd like to just sleep through it all
When bad times become even worse.
I have nothing left to do, nothing
Left to say.
Hiding emotions is not the best step
For one to take, God knows I've
Tried it all too much before.
Just let me sleep through all the
Injustice and all the unnecessary
Violence.
Crime and punishment run rampant
Through my mind.
I must get these pressing feelings
To stop before I become part of
Their nasty collective.
Please allow me to close my eyes
And hide myself from this world
Of cruelties; all the torment is
Too much the same.
Have you forgotten

My name and why

I exist today?

But none of that should matter, just

So long that I get the rest I so

Rightfully deserve.

1/2/01

Come Here

You say that your name has been
Mentioned here before, but I don't
Recall ever having heard it uttered
In the realm of presence.
Come here, little boy;
Come farther and tell me what
You're all about.
We've got ourselves all day,
So there is no price to pay.
Here, have some tea on the account,
Young child, you do shame to me by
Lurking in the doorway and ignoring
My plea.
I'm only an old lady here to do you
No harm; do not be afraid of my cats,
They've all had something to eat,
And they don't fancy to feast on little boys.
Come, I've many great servants and
A large room full of toys.
You can stay here all day if you

Want to; I'll call home to your parents

And tell them not to expect you

Home for dinner.

My caterers shall prepare you a fine

Plate full of the best

Or we could go driving;

I can call up the chauffeur.

See the nice, beautiful countryside

All the pretty trees grown by the road.

Or if you like animals, I can let the

Dogs out of the kennel to play.

I have many balls and sticks that

Can be thrown to them; good exercise

All in a day.

We can go horseback riding, I'll call

The instructors to the barn.

The weather seems lovely enough,

And the poor beasts are lonely just as I.

Oh, if you would only come here!

If you're afraid of my husband,

Fear not, he's been dead for many years.

We lived such a long time together,

Such a good man always did his

Work on time.

He was a wealthy entrepreneur,

And I have some money of my own.

But rich as I am, this heart is

Still lonely, for all the money in the world

Could never buy me a son…

1/2/01

Don't turn your head away from me

While I try to get my point across.

How rude of you to reject my argument,

Even before I have the first breath.

Just consider me an old friend and

Someone who wants to see you stay.

Constructive criticism is the best

Of all possibilities.

Disguised as the worst, I am here

To give you advice.

Do not fear what you do not understand,

For I could very well do you good

And change your fortune.

Nothing seems the same to your plain face—

The lucky prisoners you so often

Took for granted,

What do they have to say back to you?

I wonder if it's similar to the point

I try to get across.

We'll just have to wait and see…

1/17/01

The Vow

Why give yourself away, at the

Age of nineteen or twenty, when you

Have your whole life ahead of you?

So young, in love, and so foolish.

The promise to give your whole life away

In front of friends

And relatives alike—

Que pathetique!

Sacrificing happiness just

To fit into society;

It sounds like a

Stupid vow to me.

The trade-off isn't worth it because

It's only a great waste of time.

Can't people just be pleased with

The decisions

That you make, or does it

All have to result in an endless

Amount of pain?

The choice is yours

To make all alone,

Because I'm not going to help you

With this one.

So, be wise, my friend,

And do what you feel is right.

1/17/01

Head Games

Here I am, just like an open book,

For all to have and read.

Is there no escape from either of you;

Must you hover over my head

And monitor my every movement?

The answer (I can see) is affirmative,

So I advise you to get professional help

Before you drive me insane.

I did nothing that I know of to provoke you—

At least I did nothing to upset you to this point.

(Any sane person can see what I mean.)

See the tears of torment and torture

That I must wade through on a daily basis.

How cruel and unfair you sometimes treat me,

Accustomed to your pleasure and made

Only to serve your purposes.

That's all I'm good for

When you play these head games with me.

1/18/01

Before you stop the bleeding,

You have to stop the breathing.

Kill the beast while it's still here,

And you have a chance to get around.

The evil eye and the evil tentacle

Have reached out to their cause.

We all must hurry

Down to the river

To make ourselves

Forceful and to

Make ourselves known.

Now, chop off

All its fingers with

All the power you've got!

Legs and arms still pumping

Behind the sweet & sour muscles

From within.

Look up at the sky, friend,

And breathe a sigh of relief.

Your task is done for today,

So you can now go home

And rest up for tomorrow.

Oh, the morbid songs that we

Still teach our children!

1/18/01

We were afraid to come any closer;

The burning sheets have already

Gone up in smoke.

Why, oh why, did the innocents

Have to suffer?

Just because the man couldn't

Learn to control his tongue—

I can remember the days when

The elders of this village were

Treated with respect.

Not to be silenced by a sword;

We're all at the mercy of some

Power-hungry fiend, who must

Be stopped in his tracks.

We should have thought of everything before.

Now, disaster is trying to take over!

1/18/01

I know that you're going to leave,

So there's nothing I can do

But to hold on to each memory,

Until my mind turns blue.

One more chance you could give

Would mean the world to me.

I cannot hold my breath, however,

Because I knew you want to be free.

Oh, the agony has suddenly become

Too much for me to bear.

My heart has a way of telling me

To stop before I lose all hope.

One day, I know you'll hear my

Thick obsession.

Come back into my arms, and you

Shall be rewarded.

Every single movement you make

Shall be recorded in my heart.

Not enough time to ask me why,

But I know that I still love you.

1/19/01

Let it be time to

Liberate yourselves,

Flowers that blossom, and flowers

That bloom.

Anarchy and total panic have

Swept the nation 'round;

We have to take a stand and

Do something for ourselves.

Eyes wide shut and head first

Into the world,

We came kicking

And screaming all the way.

Even though

We do not like it,

We have to eventually face our

Greatest fears.

Flying all around

Us and swooping

Down in terror—

The pedals

Fall from heaven.

Oh, we should gather near and

Pay homage to the vessel.

Depart another time and watch

The rising sun,

But rain will have to fall down

And seep into our skin…

1/19/01

What is this sudden change of mind?

I go out to be liberal, but the impression

I give is just the opposite.

Equality is slowly going down the drain,

And I find out that I am slowly becoming

One of THEM.

All those who hate and do not believe,

Why must they all gather at my door?

Don't they know that I can't stand

Their type around here?

Filthy mutants they are!

I'd like to fry them all up and

Serve them hot on a platter.

Just the thought of that touches my fancy.

A shadow of myself smiling in the distance

Because I've accomplished something great.

So long to the rotten plague.

1/19/01

I'd like to know what you said,

Just for future reference,

When all my resources are

Going to turn dry, like dust.

I feel it's too late to repeat any

Of the following.

Mind scrambles, and the words flutter away,

Like little butterflies being carried

By the wind.

Here in a state of tranquility

All my senses are put to rest.

And that is all my mind has

Left to think…

1/19/01

Destination Unknown

Mindless music has
Always created
A passion for me—
Coming down the hall in
Full stereo sound,
I stop for a moment and forget
Everything I'm doing.
Total lack of control
Takes the front seat.
The pilot is ill and
Driving us all insane—
Heat and rain.
Vapor clouds my mind,
Fog and illusion
Heat and delusion.
Flying fast and
Out of control,
The music still
Plays in my head.
Destination unknown

As insanity

Comes on faster

Undergoing treatment,

Not knowing

If I'll ever get better.

1/19/01

One random slice of air

Can come from any atmosphere,

Thick as the day and sweet

As the dawn.

I hear where you're coming from,

But I do not know your name.

Frequently trying to encourage

The other side;

Just hear me out and know that

I do what I can.

It doesn't take a

Genius to understand.

Where are you?

I still did not hear you say your name.

He's coming down

The hall to get me;

I must lower my voice in fear.

You came to the right place,

And now you must let yourself inside.

Do as you please,

And make yourself at home.

Just please understand

That I am here and

Humble to be your servant.

1/19/01

Stuck in a room with a bunch

Of incompetents,

Teasing and aggravating my mind.

Perhaps the words of the *wise poet

Sum it all up accurately.

Material possessions tend to

Get in our way,

But that cannot help me in my

Current situation.

Such insolence

Will not be tolerated!

People filling their

Minds with this

Nonsense—instead

Of focusing on what

Is important.

Oh, how you anger me—

Three-horned fiend, teeth tearing

Into innocent flesh.

Behold the screams that you silence

With your very own threat of

Relentless exploitation.

We know what you're up to,

Yes, we know how to throw it all away

And make you become weak in the knees.

Just call is a special gift (that I possess)

As you fall in front of your peers.

*Wordsworth

1/19/01

Dearest friend,

My heart goes out to

Help you.

All my thoughts and prayers

Are extended to you in the highest.

May God above always treasure you

And answer your prayers on time.

No one deserves this punishment,

And no one deserves this fear.

Pain and sorrow will soon pass

Over you.

I have a feeling that it can't

Last too much longer.

So, my dearest friend, please

Hold on…

1/20/01

All the frustration is mine to deal with,

I don't know if I should just quit

Or carry myself across the starting line.

This time has come again;

Pent up anger has no place to escape.

Why do I tolerate all this nonsense?

My time is much more valuable

(Than anything else seems) to be

At the moment.

Share the emotional joy that I receive

From such relief;

Even the frustration cannot take

Away my bliss.

Deep within my heart, I have a feeling

That all is fair in love and pain.

But, one overrides the other, especially

When I shut off my brain.

1/21/01

Whose sweet love lay there 'neath

The tree by the side of the road?

Such cold weather

To be having no shelter,

And only a single blanket for keeping

Thy body warm—

Blissful slumber.

But, wait, whose carriage almost

Drove right by?

I hear her man

Giving orders to stop.

He springs out of

The car and cries

In delight!

Over to his girl and looks down

At her pretty, white face.

"My darling, are you awake?"

He slowly removes the blanket

To see that she's with child.

That could be his son inside her

Protruding stomach.

With blonde hair—

Just like his mother's.

Carrying her to the carriage and

Gently laying her down,

He will take her back to the place

From which they came.

1/21/01

I am a virgin for over six months,

And I am lonely; come over to me.

Hips full and yearning to swing.

Thighs tender and waiting to be

Caressed.

My breasts and nipples, firm and erect

Waiting for your touch (the touch).

Legs wide open, and eyes wide shut;

Have you been wanting pleasure

As much as I?

Hot and steamy, or cool and slow?

You look as if anything will work

Right for the moment.

So, bring yourself over here,

And we can do whatever we please—

Fulfilling our utmost desires

And putting away any non-essential needs.

Oh! Take my "virginity" all over again

So that we may have the sensation

On which we've been missing out.

1/22/01

Twenty-one and the impossible number

Have infected my mind with their virus.

Not only is my desire to learn the subject destroyed,

But I cringe at the mere mention of it.

Pumping up our minds with such ludicrous concepts,

Sometimes being ridiculed when I fail to get it right.

Why can't I understand these things like others?

They must think me a simpleton

With this virus in my brain.

I hear the voices laughing in my head,

Taunting me and tearing me apart,

What am I supposed to do, just take all this abuse?

Only time will tell how I handle everything

From now on…

1/23/01

I hope that you are happy,

You wretched excuse for a man.

Abusing my friend and calling it

The highlight of your day!

I hope you rot; I hope you pay

For your sins.

The punisher's looking for you

Right now, and he has a reputation

To fulfill.

All he wants to do is grant our wish

And kill the fiend who's done this.

You think I'm going to stop him;

You must be out of your mind!

Sit back and enjoy, all you wish makers

And concerned ones.

The time has come for him to rise

To this demon, I give no forewarning;

I'll utter not a single word like, "Beware!"

Let him pay for all his evil deeds,

While the avengers have a feast of his life.

1/24/01

Throw me in your cell for four hours

Every day.

No windows, just a single door,

But I won't be leaving anytime soon.

Time grows incredibly slow; heavy

Hands and heavy heads.

The dragon is screaming at us—

Telling us that we did not do our job.

And, here we're forced to consume

Massive piles of words, until they're

Ten times regurgitated.

Sick with boredom and frustration,

How much longer do I have to

Put in my time?

Other things could be done

And so much more efficient; the rest

Of my life can't depend all on you.

Still, I sit here and wish that

I was elsewhere;

That's all I can do at this time.

1/24/01

The Coldness

Snow is the cruelest form
Of punishment—
Preventing plans from happening
And taking away human lives.
Trudging through the sidewalks
In (our) misery;
We're so cold that we don't know
What to do—
All the illness associated and
Countless hospital bills.
Is there no cure for pneumonia?
Sick children lying in their beds,
Hypothermia.
We remember what happened to
The little match girl.
Had it been warm out, would she have
Survived to tell of her poverty—
Be adopted by a loving family
And get to stay inside on the most.
Dreadful of days—such as these?!

The naked people at the concentration
Camps could have stood outside and
Laughed at those Nazi pigs.
Instead, they froze to death, one more
Torture to rot in our minds.
Oh, the coldness represents hatred
And kills off the outsiders who are
Subjected to such a fate.
I can't take any more of this nonsense;
Melt this icy mentality away!
The world is here for us to enjoy,
And for this we have to be free
Of all the prejudice and hatred
That this snowy death loves to bring.
Lift up our voices and let us cry out
A fancy plea.
Yesterday should not matter, but
It has to (anyway) for the future
Generations of the world.

1/24/01

Frail weakness in my body;

I haven't eaten for days.

My ailment strikes me

At the strangest of times.

Because I have to be here,

Eyes watering from the pain.

This strange feeling in my gut—

Wanting to be somewhere safe,

Knowing that no one will bother me.

I can feel the blood run down my thighs;

My face grows ever paler with sickness

And disgust.

Sometimes praying for death

And its cold hands to "comfort" me—

Looking more and more at the time

And seeing how much I have left.

1/24/01

And you are chasing me

Through the yard in the summertime rain,

Still quite cold.

Soaking wet in shorts and a saggy T-shirt.

On the prowl, not sure if you're angry,

Or wanting.

Hungry—as some say

Colors in the sky flash from reds,

To purples, and to greens.

I'm no longer aware of my location;

I'm only here because of a dream—

Jaded, confused, and running

Breathing.

After me, running legs

Looking up at the sky, now as blue

As the water in the grass.

We have to go inside to perform

Our final note.

You, touching me on the shoulder,

And all the rest fades to black.

1/25/01

Register for the most important decision;

Choose wisely, my friend.

No lifetime celebration needs to

Be in the wrong hands.

So many paths we must travel

And so much to see on the way—

Distractions large and at hand.

Don't yield to the temptation

Because everything is worth it

In the end.

Always remember the proper order

In how to do things, and everything

Shall be fine.

Persistence be your guide.

Pride cannot fill your head

When you place your humility

In front of everything else.

The time has come to act on the registration;

May your journey be enlightened

And fulfilled with ecstasy.

1/25/01

Shooting the highlights of your life;
I've got everything on film,
Even all the black & white moments
Before your plans were developed.
Day and night shots—
Who's to compare the light to the dark?
(Your) color was not
Invented until recently—
All those photos taken within the last
Ten years.
Reflections of the past;
I can tell your mood by the lighting
And where you are
By the time of day
Standing still.
Ah, but no photo can contain your
True spirit, free wanderer,
Always marching to the beat of your
Own drum.
I could point and click at you as many
Times as I want, but those photos
Will always turn out blank.

You're running with the wind now…

1/29/01

Yelling out through screen doors,

Hoping I'll get a response.

I know that you can hear me

And see me with that mind.

A barrier is placed between us;

Could we live in

Different worlds?

(I'm) no longer right in

Front of your face,

And you're no longer near mine.

Light years could be

Present between us,

But our pasts could be

Measured by a thumb.

How do we know

When the truth finally

Comes to us?

Does it play a tone so loud that the

Whole universe can hear?

No one else may know the space

And distance between us.

The gaps of a generation just might

Not understand.

All that matters is that we know

We're separate,

And the screen door just serves as

A smaller purpose.

1/29/01

The Delivery Truck

I hear the delivery truck back up

At this time every morning.

5:55 a.m.

I hate that sound; it reminds me

Of how much sleep I didn't receive.

Knowing that the

Day is soon going

To start doesn't

Put my mind at ease.

All these things

That I have yet to do,

Starting in just a few hours

After the dawn.

I groan and pull the covers

Over my head;

Sleep had better come to me faster,

Or else I'm going to go insane!

Waiting all night just to find a

Moment of peace is not my idea

Of a positive change.

The delivery truck gets ready

To depart, barely after 6:00 a.m.

I pull the covers off my head

And close my eyes

For the remaining two hours.

1/29/01

Our relationship could be changing,

As I feel we're drifting apart.

Some things just don't feel the same anymore,

I've lost that vibrant feeling—

That radiant glow.

Everything is nearly gone because of

This change in emotion.

Gone because of the cold and restless rain,

Where do we go from here?

The road has more than one fork;

The day has more than one option.

We could stay together for one more week,

My dear, but what good would it do to us?

To move on, to experience the best of

Another world.

Perhaps that's what we should do,

Until we find ourselves

A better resolution;

I know that's what ought to be done.

1/31/01

Westward flowing is the wind today,

Silent in all other directions.

I look to my right and get into

The car.

The man patiently waits for me

Behind the wheel.

Feet, attached to long legs,

Lift themselves off the street.

I close the door and wait to be

Taken away.

As the wheels turn slowly,

The vehicle crawls down the street.

People going on

With their own lives

Are too busy to

Notice the sexy woman

In the back seat,

And the handsome man

Who's driving.

There's some tension

Going on between

The two of us.

Sparks may not fly, but they've

Certainly been ignited.

We'll have to wait

And see what happens

Further on down the road…

1/31/01

You're all going to grow older

And lose your intellectual fires.

Father, mothers, uncles, and aunts

Most of you will be.

Family values shall replace acting;

Money buys the

Rights to all your words.

Time is running down the hourglass;

Sand is smothering the greatness

Of your pasts,

But no one shall dismay.

It's all natural, and you will

Never notice it leaving.

Your minds will be too occupied

With dinner parties and chats with

Uncle Sal.

Too late.

You would have

Already lost it by then,

Flames reduced down to smoke

And ash of distant memories past.

Then all of you may smile because

You're content with this

Duller way of life.

1/31/01

I've often had fantasies about hitting you

And putting you in your place, below the

Ranks of all the lowest men.

Many of these fantasies were dreams, but I'd like,

Sometime, for one of them to come true,

If we ever cross paths again and you're

Just as bad as (you were) before.

The same old wrath heated up inside

My good Christian values I will ignore,

Just for a moment, when my eyes are

Flashing red.

I'll take you down with just one fist;

It should only take a second or two.

Then I'll ask God for forgiveness,

But you need to be taught a lesson in respect.

That punch I gave should have knocked

Some sense into you and, if it didn't, you

Might as well expect to be hearing from

Something or someone much worse than me.

1/31/01

Passion's Death

The death of passion took me

For such a turn.

Down in the underworld, mourning

For my love—consumed in fire

Passion loved, and, in turn, got the love

Back from many.

Including me,

Who's known to be his

Largest fan around.

Many nights, I saw myself lying

In his arms.

The days I spent in good company

With him.

Passion's death struck me as too old,

For who now is

Ever going to love again?

His evil brother, Hatred, is trying to

Steal the throne.

And I think the people will now

Allow this kind of thing to happen.

Since no one else has

Come to take the claim.

It's such a shame about my Passion,

Who has done and lived his time.

A million eyes are going to weep!

1/31/01

I can't bear the silence anymore,

Will someone break it, please?

This time, I can't take the stand

To clear out my mind.

This time, I'm all alone,

In a room full of mute zombies.

No one here dares to take the chance

Of meeting their salvation.

I am the only one left with any originality

In my bones.

Follow me, and everything will be

All right.

Then we can all break the silence

That holds us in our prison.

1/31/01

Go ahead and bite into my flesh,

To watch the blood come out

From my shoulder.

Oh, tell me that I taste good

To your mouth—

That you haven't had a treat

Like me for years.

Am I aged so that I'm good enough

To satisfy any?

Like the finest of wine, I can

Cancel out the brain and go

Straight to the senses?

Does my blood flow so smoothly

That you can taste it in your dreams?

Just the mere thought of it gets to you,

Makes you thirst for even more!

My body, unchanging, to fulfill

Your certain needs.

The morning comes, and we must retire

To our other state of being.

1/31/01

I'm upset to find you here,

In case you didn't know.

I set a day aside for both of us

To enjoy—in pursuit of lovely weather.

Instead, I see that

You're avoiding me

In any way you can—

Way to hurt my feelings!

I gave my time up for you

This doting woman has had her

Fill with this, so doting

(On you) I'll be no more.

You've lost your chance to have a

Paradise with me.

The most obvious is true;

How can I depend

On you in the future?

Perhaps, I shouldn't at all.

A lack of communication has

Torn us apart, so uncomfortable

I shall be.

It'll take months to fully recover

From the blow that you delivered

To me…

1/31/01

Spread yourself out, so you can

Have a true reason to lie.

The transparency that I receive

Comes in no particular color.

Your sinister movements may not

Be as cunning as you think.

Open up your head and pick apart

Any words that you may find.

Only then, my friend, will you know

Where I'm coming from, so ask me

No more questions pertaining to the matter.

My mouth is closed, and my shields

Are up to anything else that you decide

To throw my way.

It's all over for now, until it finally

Occurs to you that the light can only

Be seen from within.

1/31/01

Ground's being consumed in flames.

Don't you know what you're looking for?

I'm right here in between the clusters

Of these trees; try to catch me if you

Think you can.

Free yourself from the clutches

Of the leader,

Controlling the crowd with his

Once-superior glare.

I am lost and in need discovery,

My scent delivered straight to your nose.

(You're) drowning in the sweetest of perfumes,

Intoxicated by some kind of strange feeling—

Something that you've never felt before.

You break from the crowd and come after me

Oh, what a good, strong aroma can do!

1/31/01

Once a voice is heard,

Everything else turns to dust.

No water from a well can revive it;

Neither can the kiss from a scared rose.

That event is gone and (fictional) forever

Stuck in a time that no one can return to.

It's a shame that bias opinions take up

So much of our time.

All things should be seen according to

One eye.

The perfect organ shall give us

An honest view—

Clearest of everything clear.

The best containing no flaw

No one should be denied that privilege;

The right is given to all.

1/31/01

I found a piece of the mirror

That everyone claimed they had

Shattered years in the past

And given to no one.

Have a piece of your life back

On my account.

No need to thank me now,

The rations keep growing shorter,

Like the lines grow longer to

Collect a piece of this relic,

But, it has no true value at all.

Why even bother with such a

Useless item when real spending

Money can get you even more?

No arguments from the gentry,

Everything is so brand new—

Plain and reserved for the

Common folk to see.

When will we ever learn that relics

Do not exist?

1/31/01

I hold in my hand a fragile

Piece of bread.

And, I do it ever so gently,

As not to crumble the

Basis of life—

Splitting it up into little

Fragments, ready to be

Consumed by the hungry

Mouths of society.

They try to drink the water

Of youth, but they can't even

Get crumbs from the bread.

All is protected from the

Greedy lips of people

Stored behind

Lock and key.

We always want everything we

Can't have.

Immortality being

The main factor

To a happiness that we

Can never achieve.

Not in this life, not in

This state of being.

The piece of bread is

Still in my hand,

But no one could ever reach me

Behind the glass.

1/31/01

Did you know that a man once cut off his hand

And threw it to some land that he claimed

To be his own?

The drastic measures people take to claim something,

Is there a point where we should draw the line?

Altering the extremities of our bodies,

Just to obtain a solid piece of land.

How barbaric is our species that we must

Always cut off our own hands?

The temples and the spirit holders don't matter

As much as they should.

God gave them to us all for a reason, to keep

Them pure and clean,

And we're supposed to take care of ourselves,

Keep intact everything that we can—

Organs to take us out of today.

2/1/01

Eating out of other people's hands

Has caused my mind to ask the question "why'?

They feel that they have to provide me

With only the best that money can afford.

No one else can give it to me, but I want to have

These things for myself.

I severed the hands of the others so that they could

Not reach MY goal!

Selfish as you want to say it is.

My motives are different, so just shut your mouths,

And keep them that way.

I did not ask for your input, so right now, you have no say.

Come back to me later when all is said and done;

I may let you speak for a short time

About the things that should have been.

2/1/01

Be very still and very silent.

Private eyes are watching you

And recording your every move;

Try to avoid them anytime you can!

They're here to take control of your life.

No mercy; you must do as I say

Get everything of yours together

And run far, far away.

(No ruse of mine could be so strong.

What kind of purpose do you think

That it would serve?

I get no sick pleasure in telling people

Such lies.)

But, you must get out before any serious

Damage is done.

No time to turn back and ask questions

To yourself.

Everything is vital, so take advantage

As it still lies.

2/1/01

<u>If</u> you decide that it would be best

To (pick up) and leave, (then) I hold no

Further dispute.

Besides, I feel that you never (have) really

Loved me, so this makes the point

Almost moot.

Still, I wonder why you decided

To stay this long and act on your torments.

Did you think that it would impress me,

As crazy as the idea seems?

If I was the cause of your unhappiness,

I would have preferred that you'd

Have let me know.

Now, I've wasted half my time with you;

I could have done something more

Constructive.

I could have moved on to better my life.

Now it's going to take so much longer

To get back from where I left off.

  I hope that you are satisfied!

2/1/01

You give me such liberation!

I find nothing hard to believe.

A positive influence on my

Recovering mind—

Nothing demeaning have you

To say to me.

Always some positive remarks

Are new to add to my collection.

Not knowing what to do with myself,

But, for once, it's a good feeling

To have a person like you to

Believe in me is such a reward

In itself.

A man of high class and high society

Who's not condescending; what a

Fine gem to possess.

Every night, I thank God for you,

Because (every night) you give me

New hope.

2/1/01

<u>Don't</u> tell me what you think

That I cannot see!

Are you in my mind, do you have

Any idea what it's like to be me?

I think not because I'm a separate

Piece of a walking structure—

Not bound to any parts of you.

Even the good qualities that

You're known for do not

Exist within me.

I have plenty of room for my own;

Our minds can't be that similar.

Here's to different thoughts

On things about life.

It would be boring if I shared all

Your views.

But, you still can't say that you

Know all of mine.

How arrogant of you to assume!

2/1/01

Recall the images that claim

To haunt you during the night.

We've got news for them because

They're not real.

What is real anymore?

The concept is so vague to me—

Intangible objects hovering over

Our heads,

Afraid of a concept or emotion?

This is an irrational

Fear of the unknown.

We need time to check on our sanity

And all the things we seem to have

Left behind.

No mention of how we lived before

When these things

Started to frighten us.

It's just always been there,

Like the sky and

The earth and the sun.

But, we can't get rid of these things.

Nothing can be that easy,

And we'll just have to hope

That everything all goes away.

2/1/01

You hide your own cruel nature

Just to make an impression on me,

But I can see right through your bones

And skin.

I'm not like the women you've had

In your power before.

They were much easier to manipulate

And not too hard to control.

Alas, they paid their price, but thank

God they were saved!

I won't be as easy to make fall,

Try and try as you may.

My power is intimidating;

Your secretly cower in the corner

Because you're afraid that you might lose.

After all this time you thought out

Your plans.

Your scheming will do you no good.

Give up! That's the only true option

You have before you get yourself turned in.

2/1/01

<u>Have</u> you seen the reason why

I forgot to give you my regards?

I must have lost my mind that day,

Else I would have given you thanks.

The light you gave me reflects

Back on your face.

Oh, beaming, shining angel,

Do your wings still grow every night?

Shedding the feathers of the old day

And bringing forth the new.

You always put a fresh face on to

Brighten up the darkest rooms.

There's nothing that you wouldn't

Do for me, and it makes my mind feel at ease.

But I wish that I thought to thank you

Because the guilt has been with me for days.

How could I deny such a fine angel

Of his rewards?

Lord knows that I didn't mean to do it,

And I will never forget you again.

2/1/01

No shadows can lurk from behind the corner,

Unless you mind allows them to.

Just a figment of your imagination

Feeding weak thoughts into the fire,

Igniting the terrible flame.

And those who are helpless have no

Means of escape.

However, you control them,

And make everything go according to

(Your) will.

The scary images will cease to exist,

And the mental bliss will all go away.

I only know all this from experience,

So you have no need to question me

From doubt.

The day to day monsters fuel up on

Negative energy, and anxiety is their

Favorite course.

Only you can prevent their consumption;

Only you can take away the fear.

2/1/01

<u>Time</u> and essence,

Can you see the value of both?

While one allows us to heal from pain,

The other gives us our priorities.

Set straight the manner in which

We hold together the medicine from within.

No one knows the secret of the universe,

But everyone has a name.

And that name is going to give us power

To light up the darkest of chambers.

The cosmos will bow down to us if

We don't break our necks trying to look.

Time can no longer be an enemy,

Unless we perceive it as a negative connotation.

Essence excludes things such as these,

And it should because none of it's important.

2/2/01

<u>To</u> be held in the arms of sympathy

Would do me well at this time.

This day did not turn out so great,

And I am tired of this mess.

Why can't everything go faster

When I want to get through all this

Nonsense?

Wading through the muck and mire

Can only damage my lungs.

My body cannot take such abuse,

And it needs lots of time to take rest.

Warding off the impurities of the day

Has become my favorite activity.

Oh, sympathy, let me partake of this

Wonderful pleasure.

A few good days of rest shall heal

My lungs again.

2/2/01

<u>Ask</u>, and you shall be answered

The questions were given to us all.

Just pick out the form of the most

Pleasing dish.

Your wish shall be granted;

All troubles are removed.

We'll make this as easy as we can,

And nothing can hold us back

From our dreams.

As much as anyone can try to enforce

Their laws, we have the power

To resist them.

We'll give it everything we've got

Because we are persistent.

The answers shall remain free

And true to inquiring minds.

So, my friend, feel as if you can ask me

Anything.

I guarantee your satisfaction with

The sound of every word.

2/2/01

<u>Of</u> death and punishment,

All words came to cease.

My sentence is extended for

Another two years.

When am I able to get some peace?

I find that I still have to pay,

As if things weren't brutal enough.

My penance has

Lasted me for hours

Through the horror and trial of blood—

Wishing I could leave this place

So that I can use my freedom.

The relentless guards are still

Poking me with their sticks,

Enjoying every single second

Of pain that they inflict.

Those bastards,

They seem to have

No morale!

Especially seeing

The women and

Children suffer by disposing of

All the men first.

Behold the lowest form

Of all human life.

They will keep on going,

Until their motives run dry.

2/2/01

<u>Me</u>, that's the word which never

Comes to mind.

All these years short-lived;

Take advantage of the opportunity.

My crimes should already have

Been paid for.

I lived all this life for the

Benefit of others.

Isn't it time that I started to

Think about my needs?

Even others have been telling me

What I should

Have told myself—

Future advice to be taken,

But the hands on the clock

Never move forward.

Stuck in the same

Frame of mind—

And too set in my

Ways to ever use

The escape key?

Stupidity or stubbornness,

Just call it what you may.

Maybe, one day,

You'll be surprised,

And I'll turn around to

Face the other way.

2/2/01

<u>Any</u> meaning can go deeper in thought.

Why settle for the simplest interruption

When you can have the best, single

Slice of knowledge?

Go on and see what's out there so you

Have some room for some confusion.

It'd be a shame to limit yourself so soon,

When all is not seen to consume.

Senses are important, my dear, so use them

To their fullest extent—

Content because you finally found some

Expert opinion.

And, now, I can't say that you have

Never tried.

Waiting to tell me that it's time to

Let go of the point.

I have no argument there, but we

Shall never go our separate ways!

2/2/01

<u>Truth</u> is not seen as a certain

Type of color—

Splattered on a paper and looked at

By many.

Analyzed and shipped

Off to some home

Across the globe—

Studied to death and paid for

By large sums of money.

You cannot obtain truth this way!

No piece of paper

Has the right words.

Your insight is so much better

When it comes to universal topics

Such as these.

We have emotions to override the

Legalities, which seem to make

Less sense than it all.

Surrealistic mentions of metaphors,

Can truth be

Seen in any of these?

Only if the mind has a certain

Bias toward the piece;

We will never find out until we get there.

2/2/01

When will you come back to me,

My darling, little Nicky?

A year ago, we promised to

Unite our souls; you said you'd

Be back in my arms.

But, that time has passed,

And six months have followed

Since then.

Not a word I've heard from you

Since we made that vow.

Now I sit here, weeping with our son

Of six months, sitting on my lap.

You never got to see him, Nicky,

You never got to hear him cry,

And words will form

From his mouth

In another year or so.

He'll ask me for his father,

And I'll have to say, "I don't know."

The poor, broken family, separated

From his head.

Oh, please, Nicky,

Come back to me real soon.
We'll be sitting right here
By the fire,
Watching and waiting with
Our hearts.

2/2/01

About the Author

Jen Selinsky was born in 1978 in Pittsburgh, PA. She was raised in Cranberry Township. In December 2004, Jen earned her MLS from Clarion University of Pennsylvania. She now lives in Sellersburg, IN.

Some of Jen's short works have been published in several anthologies, including *The Raider Review*, *Tobeco*, and *Essence of a Dream*, published by The National Library of Poetry—for which two of her poems, "Ode to the Forest" and "Realization," won an editor's choice award. One of her works was also recently published in *The Poetry Review.com*.